SPINOSAURUS

By Susan H. Gray

The Child's World

Published in the United States of America by The Child's World®
PO Box 326, Chanhassen, MN 55317-0326
800-599-READ
www.childsworld.com

Content Adviser:
Peter Makovicky,
PhD, Curator,
Field Museum,
Chicago, Illinois

Photo Credits: Yann Arthus-Bertrand/Corbis: 8; Jonathan Blair/Corbis: 23, 25; Ric Ergenbright/Corbis: 27; Courtesy of Universal Studios/Getty Images: 10; the Granger Papers Project: 11, 13; Todd Marshall: 4, 6; The Natural History Museum, London: 7, 16, 18, 20; Joe Tucciarone/Science Photo Library/Photo Researchers, Inc.: 9; Christian Darkin/Science Photo Library/Photo Researchers, Inc.: 17; Christian Jegou/Publiphoto/Photo Researchers, Inc.: 21; Francois Gohier/Photo Researchers, Inc.: 22; University of Pennsylvania Gazette, July/August 2001, and Paläontologisches Museum München: 12, 14.

The Child's World®: Mary Berendes, Publishing Director

Editorial Directions, Inc.: E. Russell Primm, Editorial Director; Katie Marsico, Associate Editor; Ruth Martin, Line Editor; Judith Shiffer, Assistant Editor; Matt Messbarger, Editorial Assistant; Susan Hindman, Copy Editor; Melissa McDaniel, Proofreader; Olivia Nellums, Fact Checkers; Tim Griffin/IndexServ, Indexer; Dawn Friedman, Photo Researcher; Linda S. Koutris, Photo Selector

Original cover art by Todd Marshall

The Design Lab: Kathleen Petelinsek, Design and Page Production

Library of Congress Cataloging-in-Publication Data
Gray, Susan Heinrichs.
  Spinosaurus / by Susan H. Gray.
    v. cm. — (Exploring dinosaurs)
  Includes bibliographical references and index.
  Contents: Going fishing—What is a Spinosaurus?—Who discovered Spinosaurus?—Why did Spinosaurus have that sail?—What did Spinosaurus eat?—Still looking for Spinosaurus.
  ISBN 1-59296-234-3 (lib. bdg. : alk. paper) 1. Spinosaurus—Juvenile literature.
[1. Spinosaurus. 2. Dinosaurs.] I. Title.
  QE862.S3G6956 2005
  567.912—dc22   2003027052

TABLE OF CONTENTS

CHAPTER ONE

GOING FISHING

Spinosaurus (SPY-no-SAWR-uhss) stood absolutely still at the lake's edge. The water came up to his knees and lapped gently against his leathery skin. The dinosaur's long, narrow head was

Spinosaurus's *terrifying claws, sharp teeth, and high level of intelligence made it a ferocious hunter.*

lowered. His eyes, unblinking, stared into the water. He did not move a muscle.

Two enormous dragonflies swooped overhead, one right behind the other. Their huge wings made a loud whirring sound. But the noise did not bother *Spinosaurus.* He stood as still as a rock.

The sun was behind the big dinosaur, and he cast a shadow on the lake. After a few minutes, a fish swam into the shaded area. It paused for a second and then zipped away. A moment later, another fish glided into the shade. Its silvery back caught the dinosaur's eye. The heart of the big **reptile** began to beat a little faster. Yet, he stood still like a statue.

The fish turned and began to slowly swim away. Suddenly, faster than a lightning bolt, *Spinosaurus* shot his head into the water. Then he lifted it into the air. The fish thrashed violently in the dinosaur's

Unlike many larger dinosaurs, Spinosaurus was able to move at swift speeds.

mouth, but *Spinosaurus* held on tight. He turned his head upwards,

opening his jaws. The fish disappeared down the dinosaur's throat.

Spinosaurus stood quietly for a few seconds and then lowered his

head. Again, his unblinking eyes peered into the water. He did not

move a muscle.

CHAPTER TWO

WHAT IS A *SPINOSAURUS*?

Spinosaurus was a dinosaur that lived from about 100 million

to 93 million years ago. Its name is taken from the Latin

word *spina,* which means "thorn" or "spine," and the Greek word

sauros, which means "lizard." The name refers to a series of tall

spines rising from the

dinosaur's backbone.

Spinosaurus was gigantic.

In fact, it may have been the

longest meat-eating animal

to ever walk the earth. An

adult grew to be almost 50

feet (15 meters) in length.

Spinosaurus *(shown here) was not the only dinosaur with an interesting back.* Stegosaurus *(STEG-oh-SAWR-uhss) was a plant eater whose back had a row of pointed plates.* Ankylosaurus *(AN-kuh-low-SAWR-uhss) had a back that was covered by armor-like plates.*

The dinosaur's spines added greatly to its height. When *Spinosaurus* stood upright, the top of its back measured about 18 feet (5.5 m) from the ground. The animal weighed as much as 5 tons.

The reptile's skull was 5 to 6 feet (1.5 to 1.8 m) long. *Spinosaurus*'s head was narrow like that of a crocodile, and the dinosaur had powerful muscles that could snap the jaws shut in a flash. From front to back, the mouth was filled with straight, sharp teeth.

Like a crocodile's head, Spinosaurus's head was quite narrow and was filled with many sharp teeth that were perfect for cutting.

Scientists believe Spinosaurus *moved quickly on its two gigantic hind legs. It is possible to estimate* Spinosaurus's *speed by comparing fossilized dinosaur tracks with the creature's weight and the length of its legs.*

Spinosaurus moved on two huge legs. Its arms were much smaller, but were powerful nonetheless. Fingers and toes ended in sharp claws that were perfect for tearing flesh.

The creature had a strong, muscular neck and a heavy, thick tail.

This Spinosaurus model was used in the film Jurassic Park III, *which was shown in theatres in 2001. Not surprisingly, the dinosaur did a good job of frightening audiences!*

In addition to the dinosaur's great size and fearsome looks, it had one other outstanding feature. Running down its back, from the neck to the base of the tail, was a huge sail. The sail was held up by the row of spines that rose from the dinosaur's backbone. The shortest spines were at the neck and tail. The tallest spines were in the middle of the sail, with some reaching a height of almost 6 feet (1.8 m). Each spine was broad and flat, like a sword. Skin covered the spines, forming a web between them.

CHAPTER THREE

WHO DISCOVERED
SPINOSAURUS?

In 1912, Richard Markgraf discovered *Spinosaurus* bones.

Markgraf worked for German **paleontologist** Ernst Stromer von Reichenbach. At the time, Stromer and his team of **fossil** hunters were working in Egypt, which is located in northern Africa.

They were searching for the remains of **ancient** animals.

Over a period of several years, they were quite successful. They found the fossil remains of plants, turtles, crocodiles, fish, and dinosaurs.

Richard Markgraf searched for prehistoric fossils in Egypt in the early 1900s. Fossil hunting can be exciting and rewarding work, but it can also sometimes be frustrating, as well. Unlocking the mysteries of the past can take years of research and often involves visiting faraway places.

Ernst Stromer von Reichenbach with a dinosaur bone.

Among the dinosaur remains was a skeleton with tall, bladelike spines sticking up from the bones in its back. In 1915, Stromer wrote a paper describing this new dinosaur. He gave it the name *Spinosaurus*.

Stromer's team packed up his entire collection of fossils to send back to Germany. Stromer planned to return home and start working on them. He needed to clean the fossils, glue them back together, and figure out what kinds of animals they came from. Unfortunately, it took years for the fossils to arrive. But once they did, Stromer laid out the

Spinosaurus bones as he believed they had been positioned in the living dinosaur. He wrote about the skeleton and took pictures of it.

Everyone who saw the bones agreed that *Spinosaurus* was a most

unusual dinosaur.

Fossil hunters uncover the remains of a prehistoric turtle in Egypt during the early 1900s. Transporting such fossils was often costly, time consuming, and potentially destructive.

A TERRIBLE ENDING

Between 1911 and 1914, Ernst Stromer and his helpers worked hard in northern Africa. Some of his helpers were from Europe, and others were native Egyptians. Together, they lived and worked in an oasis in the western desert of Egypt. They found many fossils that were thought to be about 100 million years old. Once the fossil hunting ended, Stromer arranged for his finds to be shipped to Munich, Germany. Then he returned home.

Shortly afterwards, World War I broke out. Shipping the fossils became the last thing on anyone's mind, and no one sent them to Germany. When the war ended, Stromer again arranged to have his fossils shipped. Finally, in 1922, they

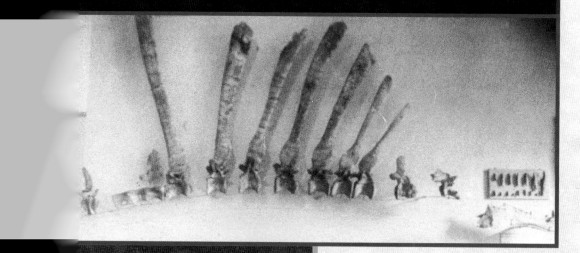

arrived in Germany. Stromer excitedly began to unpack the fossils. But when he saw them after so many years, his heart sank. Many of the fossils had been packed poorly. Some had broken to pieces on their trip from Egypt.

Nonetheless, Stromer worked hard to put them back together. It was frustrating work. Some of the fossils fell apart when they were cleaned. Some had chunks missing that Stromer *knew* had been packed. He worked long hours piecing them together, and he kept everything in a museum for safekeeping.

In 1939, World War II broke out. With bombs going off everywhere, museum workers all over Germany hurried to protect their valuables. They stashed great works of art, precious jewels, rare fossils, and many other treasures in secret hiding places. Because he refused to join the Nazis— the political party that controlled Germany at that time—Stromer's request to have his specimens moved was denied. His collection was left behind. During a bombing raid on Munich, the city's museum was demolished. Nothing was left of Stromer's fossils. His precious *Spinosaurus* skeleton had been turned to dust.

CHAPTER FOUR

WHY DID *SPINOSAURUS* HAVE THAT SAIL?

Perhaps the most unusual thing about *Spinosaurus* was its sail.

Paleontologists have several ideas about the purpose of the

structure. One idea has to do with body temperature.

Spinosaurus *undoubtedly had a unique appearance. But although it was the largest of its kind, it was not the only sail-backed dinosaur.*

Spinosaurus's sail might have helped control the dinosaur's body temperature. If cold-blooded animals lose too much body heat, they often go into a deep sleep called hibernation (HYE-bur-NAY-shuhn).

If dinosaurs were cold-blooded animals, their body temperatures

went up and down with the outside temperatures. When it was cold

outside, the reptiles' blood was cool and the animals were not very

active. When it was hot outside, the dinosaurs' blood warmed up,

and the reptiles became more active. Perhaps *Spinosaurus* stood in

the warm sun with its sail skin spread out. The blood running through the sail would warm up quickly, helping the dinosaur's body

to warm up, as well. If the dinosaur got too hot, it could stand in

the shade or turn its sail in another direction to cool off. This would

cause the body temperature to fall.

Some scientists think the sail was related to finding a mate.

Perhaps *Spinosaurus* males showed off their handsome sails to

Perhaps the sail on Spinosaurus's back helped scare off enemy dinosaurs. However, this may not have worked if the attacker was another Spinosaurus.

females. The most attractive males would have had no trouble finding mates.

Others believe the sail was used for defense. Maybe *Spinosaurus* spread its mighty sail to scare off attackers. Enemies would see that big sail and think *Spinosaurus* was even more enormous than it really was. However, some scientists say this idea doesn't make any sense. They feel *Spinosaurus* was so huge that nothing would have wanted to attack it anyway.

In recent years, some scientists have put forth one other idea. They point out that the dinosaur's spines were not thin and delicate. Instead, they were quite broad and strong. Such strong spines could have supported a thick, heavy structure. Perhaps instead of a thin sail, *Spinosaurus* had a big hump on its back. The hump might have stored fat that could have helped the dinosaur survive if it was

It is possible that Spinosaurus *ate its own kind. But what if* Spinosaurus *was hungry and couldn't readily find a meal? Maybe the dinosaur had a fat-filled hump on its back that would have helped it survive if food was scarce.*

unable to find food. Because *Spinosaurus* lived in a harsh **environment,** it may have been tough to find food. Like so many other things about dinosaurs, the mystery of *Spinosaurus*'s sail might never be solved.

SOME OTHER ANIMALS WITH SPINES

Spinosaurus was not the only animal with spines rising from its backbone. Another large sail-backed dinosaur named *Ourano-saurus* (oo-RAN-oh-SAWR-uhss) (below, right) also had them. *Ouranosaurus* lived at about the same time and in the same place as *Spinosaurus*. However, *Ouranosaurus* ate plants and was only about 24 feet (7.3 m) in length. The spines that stuck up from its backbones were flat like those of *Spinosaurus*.

Dimetrodon (dy-MET-ruh-DON) was another sail-backed animal. This reptile lived about 50 million years before dinosaurs

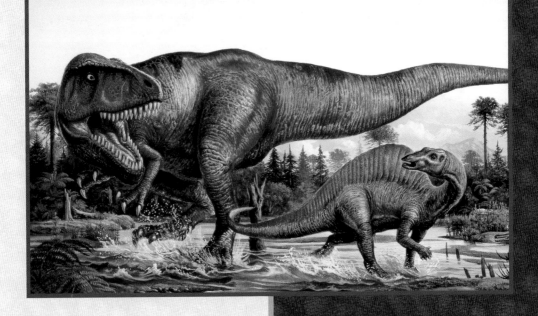

appeared on earth. *Dimetrodon* weighed more than 500 pounds (227 kilograms). It walked on four short legs, with its body close to the ground. Its sail was quite impressive, rising high above the animal's back. Its spines were slender, not broad and flat.

Some modern animals also have long spines rising from their backbones. The buffalo is a large, shaggy animal that lives on the plains of North America. Right behind its neck is a huge hump. Spines from the buffalo's backbone support the hump. The spines are broad and flat, much like those of *Ouranosaurus* and *Spinosaurus*.

CHAPTER FIVE

WHAT DID *SPINOSAURUS* EAT?

To figure out what dinosaurs ate, scientists look at the animals' teeth and bodies. Meat-eating dinosaurs were built for tracking down **prey.** Many had strong back legs and were good runners. Meat eaters also had sharp teeth for tearing flesh. Often, their teeth

Spinosaurus probably would have enjoyed feasting upon this prehistoric fish!

were **notched** and curved backwards. Plant-eating dinosaurs were usually slower, bulkier animals. They often had many dull teeth that were good for grinding down plant material.

It appears that *Spinosaurus* ate fish. Its head was long, low, and narrow—much like the head of a crocodile. A head with a narrow snout would have sliced easily through water. The dinosaur's teeth were long, straight, and pointed. They would have been excellent for grabbing and holding a struggling fish.

Spinosaurus might also have hunted land animals. And it may have dined on animals that had already died. A dinosaur cousin of *Spinosaurus* was found with fish scales within its rib cage. This shows that some relatives of *Spinosaurus* ate fish. Perhaps one day, scientists will discover a *Spinosaurus* skeleton complete with its last meal. Then we will have a better idea about what the dinosaur ate.

CHAPTER SIX

STILL LOOKING FOR *SPINOSAURUS*

Some paleontologists today are still looking for *Spinosaurus* remains. They are making trips to northern Africa, where the reptile was first found. They hope to learn more about this unusual dinosaur and its life.

However, the work is slow and difficult. It is not easy to plan a fossil-hunting trip. The first problem usually is figuring out how to pay for the trip. The scientists

Paleontologists uncovered this fossilized Dinogorgon *skull in Africa.* Dinogorgon *was a prehistoric creature that roamed Africa before dinosaurs even walked the earth. By studying the shape of its teeth, paleontologists know that* Dinogorgon *was a meat eater.*

need money to pay for travel, equipment, food, and helpers.

Before they set out, paleontologists try to learn everything about the places where they will be hunting. Will they be close to town? Where can they buy food? Where can they hire some help? What is the weather like? Will they get around by driving or by hiking? Do they need to take any special clothes, supplies, or medicine? What kinds of maps will they need? What if they make a great discovery and need more time and money to check it out?

Sometimes it is also a problem to get permission to hunt dinosaurs. Not every country will allow people to come in and look for fossils. So before paleontologists arrive, they need to discuss certain things. What if the scientists discover a new dinosaur? Can they go ahead and dig it up? Who gets to keep the skeleton? Can the scientists take the bones out of the country if they

Paleontologists continue to search Africa for additional Spinosaurus *fossils.*
Their work is challenging, but it will ultimately help us to learn more about
this mysterious sail-backed dinosaur and the world in which it lived.

promise to send them back? Many things must be decided.

Over the last few years, many paleontologists have faced these

problems. Nonetheless, some have continued to search northern

Africa. They have discovered some *Spinosaurus* teeth and a few

bones. But a complete skeleton has not yet been found. There is

still plenty of work to do.

Glossary

ancient (AYN-shunt) Something that is ancient is very old. Paleontologists study ancient life.

environment (en-VYE-ruhn-muhnt) An environment is made up of the things that surround a living creature, such as the air and soil. *Spinosaurus* lived in a harsh environment.

fossil (FOSS-uhl) A fossil is something left behind by an ancient plant or animal. Ernst Stromer and his team searched for fossils in Egypt.

notched (NOCHT) Notched describes a V-shaped cut or groove. Meat-eating dinosaurs often had notched teeth.

oasis (oh-AY-siss) An oasis is an area with plants and water within a desert. Stromer and his team worked in an oasis in a desert in western Egypt.

paleontologist (pale-ee-uhn-TOL-uh-jist) A paleontologist is a person who studies ancient living things. Paleontologists discovered the remains of a *Spinosaurus* in the early 1900s.

prey (PRAY) Prey are animals that are hunted and eaten by other animals. *Spinosaurus* hunted prey such as fish.

reptile (REP-tile) A reptile is an animal that breathes air, has a backbone, and is usually covered with scales or plates. *Spinosaurus* was a reptile.

specimens (SPESS-uh-muhnz) Specimens are things used to represent an entire group. It took a great deal of time for Stromer's dinosaur specimens to reach Germany.

Did You Know?

▸ *Spinosaurus* had a somewhat flexible back. This means that the dinosaur might have arched its back to fully spread the sail.

▸ Although other dinosaurs were sail-backed, *Spinosaurus* had the tallest sail.

▸ Some paleontologists believe *Spinosaurus* was a peaceful reptile that did not fight with or attack other dinosaurs. They believe this because *Spinosaurus* could not risk tearing its sail during a fight.

How to Learn More

AT THE LIBRARY

Barrett, Paul. *National Geographic Dinosaurs*. Washington, D.C.: National Geographic Society, 2001.

Lambert, David, Darren Naish, and Liz Wyse. *Dinosaur Encyclopedia*. New York: DK Publishing, 2001.

Palmer, Douglas, and Barry Cox (editors). *The Simon & Schuster Encyclopedia of Dinosaurs & Prehistoric Creatures: A Visual Who's Who of Prehistoric Life*. New York: Simon & Schuster, 1999.

ON THE WEB

Visit our home page for lots of links about *Spinosaurus*:

http://www.childsworld.com/links.html

NOTE TO PARENTS, TEACHERS, AND LIBRARIANS: We routinely verify our Web links to make sure they're safe, active sites—so encourage your readers to check them out!

PLACES TO VISIT OR CONTACT

AMERICAN MUSEUM OF NATURAL HISTORY
To view numerous dinosaur fossils, as well as the
fossils of several ancient animals
Central Park West at 79th Street
New York, NY 10024-5192
212/769-5100

CARNEGIE MUSEUM OF NATURAL HISTORY
To view a variety of dinosaur skeletons, as well as
fossils related to other extinct animals
4400 Forbes Avenue
Pittsburgh, PA 15213
412/622-3131

DINOSAUR NATIONAL MONUMENT
To view a huge deposit of dinosaur bones
in a natural setting
Dinosaur, CO 81610-9724
  or
DINOSAUR NATIONAL MONUMENT (QUARRY)
11625 East 1500 South
Jensen, UT 84035
435/781-7700

MUSEUM OF THE ROCKIES
To see real dinosaur fossils, as well as robotic replicas
Montana State University
600 West Kagy Boulevard
Bozeman, MT 59717-2730
406/994-2251 or 406/994-DINO (3466)

NATIONAL MUSEUM OF NATURAL HISTORY
(SMITHSONIAN INSTITUTION)
To see several dinosaur exhibits and special
behind-the-scenes tours
10th Street and Constitution Avenue NW
Washington, DC 20560-0166
202/357-2700

The Geologic Time Scale

CAMBRIAN PERIOD

Date: 540 million to 505 million years ago
Most major animal groups appeared by the end of this period. Trilobites were common and algae became more diversified.

ORDOVICIAN PERIOD

Date: 505 million to 440 million years ago
Marine life became more diversified. Crinoids and blastoids appeared, as did corals and primitive fish. The first land plants appeared. The climate changed greatly during this period—it began as warm and moist, but temperatures ultimately dropped. Huge glaciers formed, causing sea levels to fall.

SILURIAN PERIOD

Date: 440 million to 410 million years ago
Glaciers melted, sea levels rose, and the earth's climate became more stable. Fish with jaws first appeared, as did the first freshwater fish. Plants with vascular systems developed. This means they had parts that helped them to conduct food and water.

DEVONIAN PERIOD

Date: 410 million to 360 million years ago
Fish became more diverse, as did land plants. The first trees and forests appeared at this time, and the earliest seed-bearing plants began to grow. The first land-living vertebrates and insects appeared. Fossils also reveal evidence of the first ammonites and amphibians. The climate was warm and mild.

CARBONIFEROUS PERIOD

Date: 360 million to 286 million years ago
The climate was warm and humid, but cooled toward the end of the period. Coal swamps dotted the landscape, as did a multitude of ferns. The earliest reptiles walked the earth. Pelycosaurs such as *Edaphosaurus* evolved toward the end of the Carboniferous period.

PERMIAN PERIOD

Date: 286 million to 248 million years ago
Algae, sponges and corals were common on the ocean floor. Amphibians and reptiles were also prevalent at this time, as were seed-bearing plants and conifers. However, this period ended with the largest mass extinction on earth. This may have been caused by volcanic activity or the formation of glaciers and the lowering of sea levels.

TRIASSIC PERIOD

Date: 248 million to 208 million years ago
The climate during this period was warm and dry. The first true mammals appeared, as did frogs, salamanders, and lizards. Evergreen trees made up much of the plant life. The first dinosaurs, including *Coelophysis*, walked the earth. In the skies, pterosaurs became the earliest winged reptiles to take flight. In the seas, ichthyosaurs and plesiosaurs made their appearance.

JURASSIC PERIOD

Date: 208 million to 144 million years ago
The climate of the Jurassic period was warm
and moist. The first birds appeared at this
time, and plant life was more diverse and
widespread. Although dinosaurs didn't even
exist in the beginning of the Triassic period,
they ruled the earth by Jurassic times.
*Allosaurus, Apatosaurus, Archaeopteryx,
Brachiosaurus, Compsognathus, Diplodocus,
Ichthyosaurus, Plesiosaurus,* and *Stegosaurus*
were just a few of the prehistoric creatures
that lived during this period.

CRETACEOUS PERIOD

Date: 144 million to 65 million years ago
The climate of the Cretaceous period was
fairly mild. Many modern plants developed,
including those with flowers. With flowering
plants came a greater diversity of insect life.
Birds further developed into two types: flying
and flightless. Prehistoric creatures such as
*Ankylosaurus, Edmontosaurus, Iguanodon,
Maiasaura, Oviraptor, Psittacosaurus, Spinosaurus, Triceratops, Troodon, Tyrannosaurus rex,*
and *Velociraptor* all existed during this period.
At the end of the Cretaceous period came a
great mass extinction that wiped out the
dinosaurs, along with many other groups
of animals.

TERTIARY PERIOD

Date: 65 million to 1.8 million years ago
Mammals were extremely diversified at this
time, and modern-day creatures such as hors-
es, dogs, cats, bears, and whales developed.

QUATERNARY PERIOD

Date: 1.8 million years ago to today
Temperatures continued to drop during this
period. Several periods of glacial development
led to what is known today as the Ice Age.
Prehistoric creatures such as glyptodonts,
mammoths, mastodons, *Megatherium,* and
sabre-toothed cats roamed the earth. A mass
extinction of these animals occurred approxi-
mately 10,000 years ago. The first human
beings evolved during the Quaternary period.

Index

About the Author

Susan H. Gray has bachelor's and master's degrees in zoology and has taught college-level courses in biology. She first fell in love with fossil hunting while studying paleontology in college. In her 25 years as an author, she has written many articles for scientists and researchers, and many science books for children. Susan enjoys gardening, traveling, and playing the piano. She and her husband, Michael, live in Cabot, Arkansas.